PEANUTS®
MAD LIBS®

by Mickie Matheis

PSS!
PRICE STERN SLOAN
An Imprint of Penguin Random House

PRICE STERN SLOAN
Penguin Young Readers Group
An Imprint of Penguin Random House LLC

Mad Libs format copyright © 2015 by Price Stern Sloan, an imprint of Penguin Random House LLC. All rights reserved.

Concept created by Roger Price & Leonard Stern

© 2015 Peanuts Worldwide LLC

Published by Price Stern Sloan, an imprint of Penguin Random House LLC, 345 Hudson Street, New York, New York 10014. Printed in the USA

ISBN 978-0-8431-8331-3
1 3 5 7 9 10 8 6 4 2

MAD⊙LIBS®
INSTRUCTIONS

MAD LIBS® is a game for people who don't like games!
It can be played by one, two, three, four, or forty.

• RIDICULOUSLY SIMPLE DIRECTIONS

In this tablet you will find stories containing blank spaces where words
are left out. One player, the READER, selects one of these stories. The
READER does not tell anyone what the story is about. Instead, he/she asks
the other players, the WRITERS, to give him/her words. These words are
used to fill in the blank spaces in the story.

• TO PLAY

The READER asks each WRITER in turn to call out a word—an adjective or
a noun or whatever the space calls for—and uses them to fill in the blank
spaces in the story. The result is a MAD LIBS® game.

When the READER then reads the completed MAD LIBS® game to the other
players, they will discover that they have written a story that is fantastic,
screamingly funny, shocking, silly, crazy, or just plain dumb—depending
upon which words each WRITER called out.

• EXAMPLE (*Before* and *After*)

"_____ !" he said _____
           EXCLAMATION   ADVERB

as he jumped into his convertible _____ and
                                              NOUN

drove off with his _____ wife.
                          ADJECTIVE

"_____*Ouch*_____ !" he said _____*stupidly*_____
           EXCLAMATION   ADVERB

as he jumped into his convertible _____*cat*_____ and
                                              NOUN

drove off with his _____*brave*_____ wife.
                          ADJECTIVE

In case you have forgotten what adjectives, adverbs, nouns, and verbs are, here is a quick review:

An ADJECTIVE describes something or somebody. *Lumpy*, *soft*, *ugly*, *messy*, and *short* are adjectives.

An ADVERB tells how something is done. It modifies a verb and usually ends in "ly." *Modestly*, *stupidly*, *greedily*, and *carefully* are adverbs.

A NOUN is the name of a person, place, or thing. *Sidewalk*, *umbrella*, *bridle*, *bathtub*, and *nose* are nouns.

A VERB is an action word. *Run*, *pitch*, *jump*, and *swim* are verbs. Put the verbs in past tense if the directions say PAST TENSE. *Ran*, *pitched*, *jumped*, and *swam* are verbs in the past tense.

When we ask for A PLACE, we mean any sort of place: a country or city (*Spain*, *Cleveland*) or a room (*bathroom*, *kitchen*).

An EXCLAMATION or SILLY WORD is any sort of funny sound, gasp, grunt, or outcry, like *Wow!*, *Ouch!*, *Whomp!*, *Ick!*, and *Gadzooks!*

When we ask for specific words, like a NUMBER, a COLOR, an ANIMAL, or a PART OF THE BODY, we mean a word that is one of those things, like *seven*, *blue*, *horse*, or *head*.

When we ask for a PLURAL, it means more than one. For example, *cat* pluralized is *cats*.

MAD LIBS® is fun to play with friends, but you can also play it by yourself! To begin with, DO NOT look at the story on the page below. Fill in the blanks on this page with the words called for. Then, using the words you have selected, fill in the blank spaces in the story.

Now you've created your own hilarious MAD LIBS® game!

THE PEANUTS GALLERY

ADJECTIVE _____

A PLACE _____

NOUN _____

PART OF THE BODY _____

NOUN _____

ADJECTIVE _____

ADJECTIVE _____

ANIMAL _____

SILLY WORD _____

NOUN _____

NOUN _____

PART OF THE BODY _____

NOUN _____

SILLY WORD _____

TYPE OF FOOD _____

PERSON IN ROOM (MALE) _____

CELEBRITY (MALE) _____

NOUN _____

MAD LIBS®

THE PEANUTS GALLERY

The Peanuts are a/an **Skylanders** gang of youngsters growing up
in (the) **Skylands**. The main character of this group is a/an
Skylander named Charlie Brown. He is known for his large, bald
head, the yellow **chest** with a black zigzag that he
wears, and his habit of saying "**mom** grief" whenever he's
feeling frustrated or **hungry**. Charlie Brown lives with his
parents, his little sister, Sally, and his pet **donkey** named
poopy. He has a best **frend** named Linus who
carries around a security **toilet** and sucks his **toes**
whenever he needs to think or calm down. Lucy is Linus's sister,
and she can be a very crabby **girl** when she's not pleased,
shouting things like "Blockhead!" and "**Skylosen**!"
crasy Patty is another friend of Charlie Brown's. Her
nickname for him is **(nud**, and she thinks he's as
handsome as **Lucfingobon**! Unfortunately for Patty, Charlie Brown
only thinks of her as a/an **frend**.

From PEANUTS MAD LIBS® • © 2015 Peanuts Worldwide LLC. Published by Price Stern Sloan,
an imprint of Penguin Random House LLC, 345 Hudson Street, New York, NY 10014.

MAD LIBS® is fun to play with friends, but you can also play it by yourself! To begin with, DO NOT look at the story on the page below. Fill in the blanks on this page with the words called for. Then, using the words you have selected, fill in the blank spaces in the story.

Now you've created your own hilarious MAD LIBS® game!

WRITE ON, SNOOPY

ADJECTIVE _____

NOUN _____

ADJECTIVE _____

NOUN _____

VERB _____

TYPE OF FOOD _____

NOUN _____

PART OF THE BODY _____

PLURAL NOUN _____

ADJECTIVE _____

ADJECTIVE _____

ANIMAL _____

NOUN _____

PART OF THE BODY (PLURAL) _____

MAD LIBS

WRITE ON, SNOOPY

Snoopy fancies himself a/an _____ author and can often
ADJECTIVE

be found writing the Great American _____ on top of his
NOUN

doghouse. His favorite opening line is: "It was a dark and _____
ADJECTIVE

night." Here are some other options he considered:

- An enormous _____ came thundering toward him, and if
NOUN

  he didn't _____ immediately, he would be trampled as flat
VERB

  as a/an _____.
TYPE OF FOOD

- When the mysterious _____ put on a fake _____
NOUN   PART OF THE BODY

  and a pair of dark _____, the world knew him as
PLURAL NOUN

  "Joe _____."
ADJECTIVE

- I knew that my life would never be the same the moment that

  _____ _____ moved in next door.
  ADJECTIVE   ANIMAL

- As the World Famous Tennis Ace slammed the yellow _____
NOUN

  over the net to win the game, the crowd went wild, cheering and

  stomping their _____.
PART OF THE BODY (PLURAL)

From PEANUTS MAD LIBS® • © 2015 Peanuts Worldwide LLC. Published by Price Stern Sloan,
an imprint of Penguin Random House LLC, 345 Hudson Street, New York, NY 10014.

MAD LIBS® is fun to play with friends, but you can also play it by yourself! To begin with, DO NOT look at the story on the page below. Fill in the blanks on this page with the words called for. Then, using the words you have selected, fill in the blank spaces in the story.

Now you've created your own hilarious MAD LIBS® game!

LET'S KICK IT

ADJECTIVE _____

FIRST NAME (MALE) _____

CELEBRITY _____

VERB _____

ADJECTIVE _____

ADJECTIVE _____

PART OF THE BODY _____

ADVERB _____

NOUN _____

NOUN _____

PART OF THE BODY _____

VERB ENDING IN "ING" _____

EXCLAMATION _____

NUMBER _____

NOUN _____

MAD○LIBS®

LET'S KICK IT

There's nothing that Lucy loves to do more on a crisp, _____
_____ADJECTIVE_____

fall day than hold a football for Charlie Brown to kick. Let's

listen in to the play-by-play from commentators _____ "Mr.
_____FIRST NAME (MALE)_____

Touchdown" Smith and "The Endzoner," _____:
_____CELEBRITY_____

Mr. Touchdown: This is a do-or-_____ moment for
_____VERB_____

_____ ol' Charlie Brown.
__ADJECTIVE__

Endzoner: Yes, it is! Will he be the _____ hero—or will he
_____ADJECTIVE_____

fall flat on his _____?
__PART OF THE BODY__

Mr. Touchdown: The crowd is so _____ quiet, you could
_____ADVERB_____

hear a/an _____ drop. Lucy's holding the _____
_____NOUN_____   _____NOUN_____

steadily with the tip of her _____.
_____PART OF THE BODY_____

Endzoner: Charlie Brown's off and _____! He's just
_____VERB ENDING IN "ING"_____

about to reach the ball!

Mr. Touchdown: _____! Lucy pulled it away—and poor
_____EXCLAMATION_____

Charlie Brown sails _____ feet into the air!
_____NUMBER_____

Endzoner: The kick is *not* good! And the _____ goes wild!
_____NOUN_____

MAD LIBS® is fun to play with friends, but you can also play it by yourself! To begin with, DO NOT look at the story on the page below. Fill in the blanks on this page with the words called for. Then, using the words you have selected, fill in the blank spaces in the story.

Now you've created your own hilarious MAD LIBS® game!

GOOD GRIEF!

PART OF THE BODY (PLURAL) _____

ADJECTIVE _____

NOUN _____

TYPE OF LIQUID _____

NOUN _____

NOUN _____

NOUN _____

PERSON IN ROOM _____

ADJECTIVE _____

VERB ENDING IN "ING" _____

VERB ENDING IN "ING" _____

PART OF THE BODY _____

MAD LIBS®

GOOD GRIEF!

The Peanuts gang will roll their _____ skyward and
<u>PART OF THE BODY (PLURAL)</u>

mutter "Good grief!" whenever things are going from bad to

_____ , like in these instances:
<u>ADJECTIVE</u>

- Charlie Brown says it whenever Sally makes ridiculous comments to

  him—like how the _____ Ocean is the largest body of
  <u>NOUN</u>

  _____ in the world.
  <u>TYPE OF LIQUID</u>

- Schroeder says it whenever Lucy leans on his prized _____and
  <u>NOUN</u>

  insists that one day they will be husband and _____.
  <u>NOUN</u>

- The World War I Flying _____ says it whenever
  <u>NOUN</u>

  _____ , aka the Red Baron, shoots holes in his
  <u>PERSON IN ROOM</u>

  _____ airplane.
  <u>ADJECTIVE</u>

- Peppermint Patty says it when she is sent to the principal's office for

  _____ in class.
  <u>VERB ENDING IN "ING"</u>

- Snoopy thinks it whenever Woodstock is _____
  <u>VERB ENDING IN "ING"</u>

  upside down and smashes _____-first into Snoopy's
  <u>PART OF THE BODY</u>

  doghouse. Ouch!

From PEANUTS MAD LIBS® • © 2015 Peanuts Worldwide LLC. Published by Price Stern Sloan,
an imprint of Penguin Random House LLC, 345 Hudson Street, New York, NY 10014.

MAD LIBS® is fun to play with friends, but you can also play it by yourself! To begin with, DO NOT look at the story on the page below. Fill in the blanks on this page with the words called for. Then, using the words you have selected, fill in the blank spaces in the story.

Now you've created your own hilarious MAD LIBS® game!

WANTED: BASEBALL MANAGER

ADJECTIVE _____

ARTICLE OF CLOTHING _____

VERB ENDING IN "ING" _____

NOUN _____

ADJECTIVE _____

PERSON IN ROOM (FEMALE) _____

NOUN _____

VERB ENDING IN "ING" _____

CELEBRITY _____

ADJECTIVE _____

ADJECTIVE _____

VERB ENDING IN "ING" _____

PART OF THE BODY (PLURAL) _____

VERB _____

PART OF THE BODY (PLURAL) _____

VERB _____

MAD☺LIBS®
WANTED: BASEBALL MANAGER

Are you a/an _____ fan of America's favorite pastime? Do you
            ADJECTIVE

usually put on your mitt before your _____? Do
                                    ARTICLE OF CLOTHING

you consider pitching, hitting, and _____ to be some
                                    VERB ENDING IN "ING"

of your best skills? If so, then you might be the perfect _____
                                                          NOUN

to manage the neighborhood baseball team. This _____ group
                                               ADJECTIVE

of misfit players includes _____, who plays outfield
                           PERSON IN ROOM (FEMALE)

but misses every single fly-_____ that comes her way; Snoopy,
                            NOUN

who's usually snoozing or _____ at shortstop; and
                          VERB ENDING IN "ING"

_____, who just stands there looking _____. Can
CELEBRITY   ADJECTIVE

you come up with _____ signals for the players? For example,
                 ADJECTIVE

touching your ball cap means to take off _____, and
                                         VERB ENDING IN "ING"

clapping your _____ means to _____.
              PART OF THE BODY (PLURAL)   VERB

Candidates who can also pitch get priority consideration, especially

if they are fast on their _____ and can dodge line
                          PART OF THE BODY (PLURAL)

drives! If you think the manager position could be right for you, and

you could take this struggling team to the championship, _____
                                                          VERB

today for an application!

From PEANUTS MAD LIBS® • © 2015 Peanuts Worldwide LLC. Published by Price Stern Sloan, an imprint of Penguin Random House LLC, 345 Hudson Street, New York, NY 10014.

MAD LIBS® is fun to play with friends, but you can also play it by yourself! To begin with, DO NOT look at the story on the page below. Fill in the blanks on this page with the words called for. Then, using the words you have selected, fill in the blank spaces in the story.

Now you've created your own hilarious MAD LIBS® game!

THE DOCTOR IS IN

NUMBER _____

ADJECTIVE _____

ADJECTIVE _____

VERB ENDING IN "ING" _____

PART OF THE BODY _____

VERB ENDING IN "ING" _____

PLURAL NOUN _____

NOUN _____

ADJECTIVE _____

NOUN _____

A PLACE _____

TYPE OF LIQUID _____

PART OF THE BODY _____

NOUN _____

PART OF THE BODY _____

ADJECTIVE _____

PART OF THE BODY _____

Lucy likes to help people—or at least tell them what to do. For

only _____ cents, she will listen to problems, whether big or
     NUMBER

_____, and give _____ advice. Charlie Brown
  ADJECTIVE   ADJECTIVE

can often be found _____ on the stool in front of
             VERB ENDING IN "ING"

Lucy's psychiatry booth, pouring his _____ out
                            PART OF THE BODY

to her. For example, when he told her he had a fear of

_____ _____, she informed him that he had
VERB ENDING IN "ING"   PLURAL NOUN

_____-ophobia. When he said that he was depressed and
  NOUN

_____ and that his _____ had no meaning, she told
  ADJECTIVE   NOUN

him to go to (the) _____ and have a peanut butter sandwich
           A PLACE

and a glass of _____. When he said how much he wanted
       TYPE OF LIQUID

to hold the little red-haired girl's _____, Lucy said to stop
                  PART OF THE BODY

being a wishy-washy _____ and to get off his _____
             NOUN   PART OF THE BODY

and just do it! Even though Lucy has _____ intentions, most
                         ADJECTIVE

of the time her "patients" leave shaking their _____ and
                             PART OF THE BODY

wondering why they listened to her in the first place.

MAD LIBS® is fun to play with friends, but you can also play it by yourself! To begin with, DO NOT look at the story on the page below. Fill in the blanks on this page with the words called for. Then, using the words you have selected, fill in the blank spaces in the story.

Now you've created your own hilarious MAD LIBS® game!

MY SWEET BABBOO

ADJECTIVE _____

ANIMAL _____

TYPE OF FOOD _____

PART OF THE BODY _____

VERB _____

ADVERB _____

PART OF THE BODY (PLURAL) _____

TYPE OF FOOD _____

PLURAL NOUN _____

NOUN _____

A PLACE _____

PART OF THE BODY _____

NOUN _____

VERB _____

PLURAL NOUN _____

PERSON IN ROOM (FEMALE) _____

MAD LIBS

MY SWEET BABBOO

Dear Linus:

I am so proud and _____ to call you my Sweet Babboo. I
                     ADJECTIVE

know you don't like when I call you this, but it's better than Darling

_____ or Snuggle _____, right? Do you know that I
   ANIMAL   TYPE OF FOOD

get butterflies in my _____ whenever I _____ next
                      PART OF THE BODY   VERB

to you? There are a lot of things you can do to show how _____
                                                           ADVERB

you love me. We could go to the movie theater together and hold

_____ and share buttered _____. Or you
PART OF THE BODY (PLURAL)   TYPE OF FOOD

could carry my _____ home from school. Or you could
               PLURAL NOUN

climb to the top of the highest _____ and shout to all (the)
                                NOUN

_____, "I love Sally Brown with all my _____!"
A PLACE   PART OF THE BODY

You are my _____ in shining armor, Sweet Babboo, and I
           NOUN

know someday we will _____ happily ever after!
                     VERB

Hugs and _____,
         PLURAL NOUN

_____
PERSON IN ROOM (FEMALE)

MAD LIBS® is fun to play with friends, but you can also play it by yourself! To begin with, DO NOT look at the story on the page below. Fill in the blanks on this page with the words called for. Then, using the words you have selected, fill in the blank spaces in the story.

Now you've created your own hilarious MAD LIBS® game!

KEEP CALM AND CARRY A BLANKET

ADJECTIVE _____

NOUN _____

PLURAL NOUN _____

PLURAL NOUN _____

ANIMAL _____

NOUN _____

PART OF THE BODY _____

VERB _____

PLURAL NOUN _____

PLURAL NOUN _____

ANIMAL (PLURAL) _____

PLURAL NOUN _____

VERB _____

CELEBRITY (MALE) _____

MAD☺LIBS®
KEEP CALM AND
CARRY A BLANKET

Linus's blanket makes him feel safe and _____. But this handy
<u>ADJECTIVE</u>

_____ can also be used in many other ways, such as:
<u>NOUN</u>

- A slingshot to knock _____ off fences or _____
  <u>PLURAL NOUN</u>   <u>PLURAL NOUN</u>

  from tree branches.

- A lasso to catch a galloping _____ or seize a/an
  <u>ANIMAL</u>

  _____ that's just out of reach.
  <u>NOUN</u>

- A stylish scarf to keep your _____ warm.
  <u>PART OF THE BODY</u>

- A parachute to help you _____ to safety.
  <u>VERB</u>

- A whip to keep away attacking _____.
  <u>PLURAL NOUN</u>

- A bullfighter's cape to use with charging _____.
  <u>PLURAL NOUN</u>

- An insect swatter to keep away pesky little _____.
  <u>ANIMAL (PLURAL)</u>

- A hammock to hang between two _____ so you can
  <u>PLURAL NOUN</u>

  _____ on it.
  <u>VERB</u>

- A big bow tie so you look as handsome as _____.
  <u>CELEBRITY (MALE)</u>

From PEANUTS MAD LIBS® • © 2015 Peanuts Worldwide LLC. Published by Price Stern Sloan,
an imprint of Penguin Random House LLC, 345 Hudson Street, New York, NY 10014.

MAD LIBS® is fun to play with friends, but you can also play it by yourself! To begin with, DO NOT look at the story on the page below. Fill in the blanks on this page with the words called for. Then, using the words you have selected, fill in the blank spaces in the story.

Now you've created your own hilarious MAD LIBS® game!

A DAY IN THE LIFE

VERB ENDING IN "ING" _____

VERB ENDING IN "ING" _____

ADJECTIVE _____

ADJECTIVE _____

SAME ADJECTIVE _____

ADJECTIVE _____

NOUN _____

NOUN _____

NUMBER _____

TYPE OF LIQUID _____

VERB ENDING IN "ING" _____

PLURAL NOUN _____

ANIMAL _____

NUMBER _____

NOUN _____

ADJECTIVE _____

Charlie Brown woke up to the sun brightly _____

VERB ENDING IN "ING"

in the sky and birds cheerily _____ in the trees.

VERB ENDING IN "ING"

He was hopeful that meant it would be a/an _____ day!

ADJECTIVE

But things quickly went from good to _____—and then

ADJECTIVE

from _____ to _____! First, the _____

SAME ADJECTIVE   ADJECTIVE   NOUN

that he took outside to fly around his backyard got eaten by the

kite-eating _____. After that, he went to the baseball field,

NOUN

and his team was only _____ outs away from winning the

NUMBER

championship game when suddenly the clouds opened up and

dumped down buckets of _____, sending everyone

TYPE OF LIQUID

_____ for cover and ending the game. "I can't stand it!"

VERB ENDING IN "ING"

he groaned. Later, when Charlie Brown tried to give Snoopy one bowl

full of _____ for dinner, his pet _____ insisted

PLURAL NOUN   ANIMAL

on being served cafeteria-style, with _____ bowls from which to

NUMBER

choose. "Why can't I have a normal _____ like everyone else?"

NOUN

he sighed. Poor Charlie Brown! If he didn't have _____ luck,

ADJECTIVE

he'd have no luck at all!

From PEANUTS MAD LIBS® • © 2015 Peanuts Worldwide LLC. Published by Price Stern Sloan,
an imprint of Penguin Random House LLC, 345 Hudson Street, New York, NY 10014.

MAD LIBS® is fun to play with friends, but you can also play it by yourself! To begin with, DO NOT look at the story on the page below. Fill in the blanks on this page with the words called for. Then, using the words you have selected, fill in the blank spaces in the story.

Now you've created your own hilarious MAD LIBS® game!

THE WORLD WAR I FLYING ACE

NOUN _____

TYPE OF LIQUID _____

COLOR _____

PERSON IN ROOM _____

VEHICLE _____

A PLACE _____

PLURAL NOUN _____

NOUN _____

PART OF THE BODY _____

VERB ENDING IN "ING" _____

PLURAL NOUN _____

PLURAL NOUN _____

NOUN _____

VERB _____ .

PART OF THE BODY _____

VERB _____

MAD LIBS
THE WORLD WAR I FLYING ACE

The World War I Flying _____ quaffs one last mug of
                         NOUN
_____ before taking off on another mission in pursuit
 TYPE OF LIQUID

of his archenemy, the _____ Baron, aka _____.
                          COLOR   PERSON IN ROOM

The Flying Ace will not rest until he has shot down the Baron's

_____, making (the) _____ a safer place for all the
   VEHICLE   A PLACE

good _____ who live there. He jumps into the cockpit of
      PLURAL NOUN

his Sopwith Camel and steadily holds the _____ stick while
                                            NOUN

slightly pushing the throttle with his _____. The Flying Ace
                                      PART OF THE BODY

is _____ low over enemy lines, scanning the skies for
   VERB ENDING IN "ING"

enemy _____, when suddenly, the Flying Ace spots the
       PLURAL NOUN

Red Baron coming up fast behind him. The sound of exploding

anti-_____ fills the sky! The Flying Ace's _____ is
     PLURAL NOUN   NOUN

on fire! He leaps to safety, using his parachute to slowly _____
                                                              VERB

to the ground below. "Curse you, Red Baron!" he thinks, angrily

shaking his _____ at the sky. "I'll get you one day. You can
            PART OF THE BODY

run—but you can't _____!"
                      VERB

MAD LIBS® is fun to play with friends, but you can also play it by yourself! To begin with, DO NOT look at the story on the page below. Fill in the blanks on this page with the words called for. Then, using the words you have selected, fill in the blank spaces in the story.

Now you've created your own hilarious MAD LIBS® game!

ALL ABOUT PEPPERMINT PATTY

CELEBRITY (FEMALE) _____

PERSON IN ROOM (MALE) _____

PART OF THE BODY _____

ADJECTIVE _____

ARTICLE OF CLOTHING (PLURAL) _____

ADJECTIVE _____

VERB ENDING IN "ING" _____

VERB _____

SILLY WORD _____

A PLACE _____

NOUN _____

ADJECTIVE _____

PART OF THE BODY _____

VERB ENDING IN "ING" _____

PERSON IN ROOM (FEMALE) _____

MAD LIBS
ALL ABOUT PEPPERMINT PATTY

Peppermint Patty, whose formal name is actually _____, is
<u>CELEBRITY (FEMALE)</u>

one of Charlie Brown's friends. She calls him _____ and
<u>PERSON IN ROOM (MALE)</u>

has a crush on him, but thinks he doesn't find her attractive because her

_____ is too big. This _____ tomboy is the captain
<u>PART OF THE BODY</u>   <u>ADJECTIVE</u>

of a baseball team that always beats the _____
<u>ARTICLE OF CLOTHING (PLURAL)</u>

off Charlie Brown's team. Patty is an exceptionally _____
<u>ADJECTIVE</u>

athlete, excelling at running, throwing, and _____.
<u>VERB ENDING IN "ING"</u>

She doesn't _____ too well in school, though. She hates essay
<u>VERB</u>

tests and says, "_____! I'm doomed!" every time she takes
<u>SILLY WORD</u>

one. She can't multiply, find (the) _____ on a map, or spell the
<u>A PLACE</u>

word "_____." Patty has a/an _____ habit of falling
<u>NOUN</u>   <u>ADJECTIVE</u>

asleep in class and then getting a cramp in her _____ because
<u>PART OF THE BODY</u>

of the way it bends while she's sleeping. After that, she can usually be

found _____ outside the principal's office. That's the
<u>VERB ENDING IN "ING"</u>

one part of school at which Peppermint _____ seems
<u>PERSON IN ROOM (FEMALE)</u>

to succeed!

MAD LIBS® is fun to play with friends, but you can also play it by yourself! To begin with, DO NOT look at the story on the page below. Fill in the blanks on this page with the words called for. Then, using the words you have selected, fill in the blank spaces in the story.

Now you've created your own hilarious MAD LIBS® game!

PIANO MAN

ADJECTIVE _____

FIRST NAME (MALE) _____

NOUN _____

A PLACE _____

NOUN _____

NUMBER _____

CELEBRITY (MALE) _____

ADJECTIVE _____

TYPE OF FOOD _____

ADVERB _____

NOUN _____

CELEBRITY (FEMALE) _____

ADJECTIVE _____

PART OF THE BODY (PLURAL) _____

PLURAL NOUN _____

VERB ENDING IN "ING" _____

VERB _____

MAD LIBS

PIANO MAN

My name is Schroeder, and I love playing the _____ piano.
ADJECTIVE

My hero is _____ van Beethoven. In my opinion, he was
FIRST NAME (MALE)

the greatest musical _____ who ever lived. He was born in
NOUN

(the) _____ and began playing the _____ when he
A PLACE   NOUN

was just _____ years old, studying under other great masters like
NUMBER

_____. The _____ music he composed was
CELEBRITY (MALE)   ADJECTIVE

genius! The first time I heard the _____ Sonata—which was
TYPE OF FOOD

one of his greatest works—I knew I wanted to play as _____
ADVERB

as Beethoven did! My _____ teacher, _____,
NOUN   CELEBRITY (FEMALE)

says I definitely have an ear for _____ classical music. And,
ADJECTIVE

according to her, my long, slender _____ are
PART OF THE BODY (PLURAL)

perfect for a pianist. They help me play with speed,

agility, and _____. I know if I spend enough hours a day
PLURAL NOUN

_____, someday I might _____ as brilliantly
VERB ENDING IN "ING"   VERB

as Beethoven!

MAD LIBS® is fun to play with friends, but you can also play it by yourself! To begin with, DO NOT look at the story on the page below. Fill in the blanks on this page with the words called for. Then, using the words you have selected, fill in the blank spaces in the story.

Now you've created your own hilarious MAD LIBS® game!

THE RANTS OF A LIFETIME

ADJECTIVE _____

NOUN _____

NUMBER _____

PART OF THE BODY _____

NOUN _____

NOUN _____

A PLACE _____

NOUN _____

ADJECTIVE _____

ADJECTIVE _____

PART OF THE BODY _____

VERB ENDING IN "ING" _____

PART OF THE BODY _____

VERB ENDING IN "ING" _____

VERB ENDING IN "ING" _____

MAD LIBS®

THE RANTS OF A LIFETIME

She's a/an _____ fussbudget . . . she's a bossy _____
              ADJECTIVE   NOUN

. . . she's Lucy Van Pelt! Whenever Lucy gets crabby—which is usually

_____ times a day—she gets a frown on her _____, and
    NUMBER   PART OF THE BODY

she'll give others a piece of her _____. What makes her mad?
                                         NOUN

Most things do, including:

- When people doubt that she will someday be _____ of the
                                                    NOUN

  United States or queen of (the) _____.
                                      A PLACE

- When Linus throws an ice-cold snow-_____ right into her
                                            NOUN

  _____ face.
     ADJECTIVE

- When Snoopy plants a sloppy, _____ kiss on the tip of her
                                    ADJECTIVE

  _____.
  PART OF THE BODY

- When someone is _____ in her path as she's trying
                    VERB ENDING IN "ING"

  to walk by.

- When she falls down and skins her _____.
                                      PART OF THE BODY

- When Charlie Brown is _____—and when he's *not*
                          VERB ENDING IN "ING"

  _____.
  VERB ENDING IN "ING"

MAD LIBS® is fun to play with friends, but you can also play it by yourself! To begin with, DO NOT look at the story on the page below. Fill in the blanks on this page with the words called for. Then, using the words you have selected, fill in the blank spaces in the story.

Now you've created your own hilarious MAD LIBS® game!

THE DIRT ON PIGPEN

A PLACE _____

PERSON IN ROOM _____

NOUN _____

ADJECTIVE _____

PART OF THE BODY (PLURAL) _____

ADJECTIVE _____

PLURAL NOUN _____

CELEBRITY _____

PERSON IN ROOM _____

VERB ENDING IN "ING" _____

NOUN _____

PART OF THE BODY (PLURAL) _____

PLURAL NOUN _____

VERB _____

PART OF THE BODY (PLURAL) _____

MAD LIBS®

THE DIRT ON PIGPEN

Welcome! This is *Live from (the)* _____! with your host,
<u>A PLACE</u>

_____ McChatty. Today in the studio we have Pigpen,
<u>PERSON IN ROOM</u>

a regular _____ from the neighborhood who's known
<u>NOUN</u>

for the _____ cloud of dust that collects around his
<u>ADJECTIVE</u>

_____. Let's check in with Pigpen:
<u>PART OF THE BODY (PLURAL)</u>

McChatty: Pigpen, you're as _____ as you are dusty! Where
<u>ADJECTIVE</u>

does it all come from?

Pigpen: I carry the dust and dirt of ancient kings and other noble

_____, like _____ and _____.
<u>PLURAL NOUN</u>   <u>CELEBRITY</u>   <u>PERSON IN ROOM</u>

McChatty: No way. Really?

Pigpen: No! It's from _____ down at the
<u>VERB ENDING IN "ING"</u>

_____ tracks and in the dump.
<u>NOUN</u>

McChatty: What do people do when you enter a room?

Pigpen: They'll pinch their _____closed or say, "Oh
<u>PART OF THE BODY (PLURAL)</u>

my _____, what died?" Or they'll just _____ as
<u>PLURAL NOUN</u>   <u>VERB</u>

fast as their _____ can carry them.
<u>PART OF THE BODY (PLURAL)</u>

MAD LIBS® is fun to play with friends, but you can also play it by yourself! To begin with, DO NOT look at the story on the page below. Fill in the blanks on this page with the words called for. Then, using the words you have selected, fill in the blank spaces in the story.

Now you've created your own hilarious MAD LIBS® game!

I HATE SCHOOL, BY SALLY

VERB _____

ADJECTIVE _____

PART OF THE BODY _____

NOUN _____

A PLACE _____

CELEBRITY _____

PLURAL NOUN _____

ARTICLE OF CLOTHING _____

ADJECTIVE _____

ADJECTIVE _____

TYPE OF LIQUID _____

VERB ENDING IN "ING" _____

VERB _____

NUMBER _____

A PLACE _____

NOUN _____

NOUN _____

NOUN _____

MAD LIBS®
I HATE SCHOOL, BY SALLY

The thought of going to school makes me want to _____.
                                                    VERB

It's just so stressful! There are too many _____ things
                                            ADJECTIVE

to know, but my _____ isn't big enough to hold all that
                PART OF THE BODY

information. I have no idea what the longest _____ in the
                                              NOUN

world is. I don't know who the vice president of (the) _____
                                                       A PLACE

is. Is it _____? I can't conjugate any _____. I also
          CELEBRITY   PLURAL NOUN

don't like that I have to wear my best _____ to school
                                        ARTICLE OF CLOTHING

every day. And how am I supposed to remember all the _____
                                                      ADJECTIVE

policies? What if I have to call in _____ and I miss
                                     ADJECTIVE

important information? What if there's no _____ in the
                                          TYPE OF LIQUID

drinking fountain? What if my teacher catches me _____
                                                  VERB ENDING IN "ING"

in class and makes me write "I will not _____ in class"
                                         VERB

_____ times? What if I get lost in the hallway and can't find
  NUMBER

my way back to (the) _____, or I forget the combination to
                      A PLACE

my _____? What if my mom packs me a peanut butter and
     NOUN

_____ sandwich instead of the _____ salad sandwich
  NOUN   NOUN

that I like? Good grief—it's no wonder I hate school!

MAD LIBS® is fun to play with friends, but you can also play it by yourself! To begin with, DO NOT look at the story on the page below. Fill in the blanks on this page with the words called for. Then, using the words you have selected, fill in the blank spaces in the story.

Now you've created your own hilarious MAD LIBS® game!

FINE FEATHERED FRIEND

COLOR _____

NOUN _____

PLURAL NOUN _____

VERB ENDING IN "ING" _____

NOUN _____

NOUN _____

TYPE OF LIQUID _____

ADJECTIVE _____

PART OF THE BODY _____

NOUN _____

CELEBRITY _____

PLURAL NOUN _____

ADJECTIVE _____

PLURAL NOUN _____

NOUN _____

Snoopy's best friend is a little _____ _____ named
                                     COLOR   NOUN
Woodstock. They like to spend time together doing all sorts of

activities, such as:

- Taking Woodstock's little feathered _____ camping,
                                          PLURAL NOUN
  hiking, and _____ in the woods as part of their
                VERB ENDING IN "ING"
  _____ Scout expeditions.
      NOUN

- Playing _____ hockey on the birdbath frozen solid with
              NOUN

  _____.
   TYPE OF LIQUID

- Taking naps on top of Snoopy's _____ doghouse, with
                                     ADJECTIVE
  Woodstock sleeping on Snoopy's _____.
                                  PART OF THE BODY

- Identifying what kind of _____ Woodstock is, thanks to the
                              NOUN
  Guide to Birds handbook authored by _____.
                                          CELEBRITY

- Going on picnics underneath the cool shade of the _____
                                                      PLURAL NOUN
  and dining on _____ treats like fried _____
                  ADJECTIVE   PLURAL NOUN
  and fresh _____.
               NOUN

MAD LIBS® is fun to play with friends, but you can also play it by yourself! To begin with, DO NOT look at the story on the page below. Fill in the blanks on this page with the words called for. Then, using the words you have selected, fill in the blank spaces in the story.

Now you've created your own hilarious MAD LIBS® game!

HAPPY DAY, HAPPY DANCE

ADJECTIVE _____

VERB ENDING IN "ING" _____

PART OF THE BODY (PLURAL) _____

ADJECTIVE _____

NOUN _____

PLURAL NOUN _____

ANIMAL (PLURAL) _____

VERB _____

PLURAL NOUN _____

ANIMAL _____

PLURAL NOUN _____

NOUN _____

A PLACE _____

NOUN _____

PART OF THE BODY (PLURAL) _____

MAD LIBS®
HAPPY DAY, HAPPY DANCE

When Snoopy is in a cheerfully _____ mood, he'll break into
　　　　　　　　　　　　　　　　ADJECTIVE

some happy _____. He dances so quickly, you can
　　　　　　VERB ENDING IN "ING"

barely see his _____ move! Here are moments that
　　　　　PART OF THE BODY (PLURAL)

make Snoopy burst into a/an _____ dance:
　　　　　　　　　　　　　ADJECTIVE

- The round-headed _____ brings Snoopy a supper dish full
  　　　　　　　　　NOUN

  of meaty _____.
  　　　　PLURAL NOUN

- Some winged _____ flutter by, and Snoopy wants to
  　　　　　　ANIMAL (PLURAL)

  _____ with them.
  　　VERB

- It's Be Kind to _____ Week.
  　　　　　　　PLURAL NOUN

- It's reunion weekend at the Daisy Hill _____ Farm for
  　　　　　　　　　　　　　　　　　　ANIMAL

  Snoopy's brothers and _____.
  　　　　　　　　　PLURAL NOUN

- It's Christmas, Thanksgiving, or _____ Day.
  　　　　　　　　　　　　　　NOUN

- A favorite new book, like *The Six Bunny-Wunnies Visit (the)*

  _____, comes out.
  　　A PLACE

- A cute long-eared _____ with puppy eyes and soft
  　　　　　　　　　NOUN

  _____ smiles at Snoopy.
  PART OF THE BODY (PLURAL)

From PEANUTS MAD LIBS® • © 2015 Peanuts Worldwide LLC. Published by Price Stern Sloan,
an imprint of Penguin Random House LLC, 345 Hudson Street, New York, NY 10014.

MAD LIBS® is fun to play with friends, but you can also play it by yourself! To begin with, DO NOT look at the story on the page below. Fill in the blanks on this page with the words called for. Then, using the words you have selected, fill in the blank spaces in the story.

Now you've created your own hilarious MAD LIBS® game!

THE LITTLE
RED-HAIRED GIRL

ADJECTIVE _____

CELEBRITY (FEMALE) _____

NOUN _____

PART OF THE BODY (PLURAL) _____

VERB _____

VERB _____

ADJECTIVE _____

VERB ENDING IN "ING" _____

SILLY WORD _____

PLURAL NOUN _____

ADJECTIVE _____

NOUN _____

NOUN _____

PART OF THE BODY _____

MAD LIBS
THE LITTLE
RED-HAIRED GIRL

Charlie Brown often daydreams about the _____ red-haired
_____ADJECTIVE_____

girl who goes to his school. She reminds him of a beautiful, red-headed

_____. Whenever he thinks about her, his _____
CELEBRITY (FEMALE)   NOUN

starts to beat faster, his _____ get sweaty, and he's
_____PART OF THE BODY (PLURAL)_____

unable to _____ straight. Sometimes during lunch period,
_____VERB_____

Charlie Brown thinks about going over and asking the little red-haired

girl if he can _____ next to her and eat his _____
_____VERB_____   ADJECTIVE

lunch. But he's afraid she'll burst out _____ right in his
_____VERB ENDING IN "ING"_____

face and say, "_____," crushing his hopes and _____.
_____SILLY WORD_____   PLURAL NOUN

So he always chickens out. Then Charlie Brown gets mad at himself

for being such a/an _____ coward and wishes he could crawl
_____ADJECTIVE_____

under a/an _____ and hide. He knows that if he can't even
_____NOUN_____

offer to share a/an _____ sandwich with the little red-haired
_____NOUN_____

girl, he'll never get up the nerve to ask to hold her _____!
_____PART OF THE BODY_____

MAD LIBS® is fun to play with friends, but you can also play it by yourself! To begin with, DO NOT look at the story on the page below. Fill in the blanks on this page with the words called for. Then, using the words you have selected, fill in the blank spaces in the story.

Now you've created your own hilarious MAD LIBS® game!

THE LEGEND OF THE GREAT PUMPKIN

A PLACE _____

PLURAL NOUN _____

NOUN _____

NOUN _____

A PLACE _____

PLURAL NOUN _____

ADJECTIVE _____

ADJECTIVE _____

TYPE OF FOOD _____

PLURAL NOUN _____

ADVERB _____

VERB ENDING IN "ING" _____

PLURAL NOUN _____

ADJECTIVE _____

PERSON IN ROOM (FEMALE) _____

On the afternoon of Halloween, Linus walked around (the)

_____, knocking on doors to tell all the _____
   A PLACE   PLURAL NOUN

in the neighborhood about the Great _____. He told
                                          NOUN

them how, on Halloween night, the Great Pumpkin rises from the

_____ patch and flies all over (the) _____, delivering
    NOUN   A PLACE

_____ to _____ children everywhere. Most of the
   PLURAL NOUN   ADJECTIVE

people Linus spoke with listened politely but thought he was a bit on

the _____ side. However, Sally agreed to wait with Linus in
        ADJECTIVE

the _____ patch that night. A bunch of trick-or-treaters came
     TYPE OF FOOD

by dressed as ghosts, witches, and _____. Hours passed,
                                           PLURAL NOUN

and the next thing Linus and Sally knew, it was morning. They had

fallen asleep! Sally was _____ furious that she missed both the
                              ADVERB

Great Pumpkin and the chance to go trick-or-_____.
                                                VERB ENDING IN "ING"

She told Linus that he owed her chocolate-covered _____
                                                        PLURAL NOUN

and other _____ candy. Poor Linus! There was nothing scarier
              ADJECTIVE

on Halloween than an angry _____!
                             PERSON IN ROOM (FEMALE)

MAD LIBS® is fun to play with friends, but you can also play it by yourself! To begin with, DO NOT look at the story on the page below. Fill in the blanks on this page with the words called for. Then, using the words you have selected, fill in the blank spaces in the story.

Now you've created your own hilarious MAD LIBS® game!

THE (PIANO) KEYS TO HER HEART

PART OF THE BODY _____

ADJECTIVE _____

ADJECTIVE _____

VERB _____

ADJECTIVE _____

NOUN _____

PLURAL NOUN _____

NOUN _____

ADJECTIVE _____

A PLACE _____

NOUN _____

SAME NOUN _____

PLURAL NOUN _____

CELEBRITY _____

PERSON IN ROOM _____

NOUN _____

ADJECTIVE _____

MAD LIBS®
THE (PIANO) KEYS
TO HER HEART

Lucy likes to stare at Schroeder's handsome _____ while
PART OF THE BODY

discussing their _____ future together. A typical conversation
ADJECTIVE

between the _____ couple sounds like this:
ADJECTIVE

Lucy: Will you expect me to cook and clean and _____ once
VERB

I'm your _____ wife?
ADJECTIVE

Schroeder: I certainly wouldn't expect you to relax on a comfy

_____ all day and eat chocolate-covered _____.
NOUN   PLURAL NOUN

Lucy: I want to live in a big, expensive _____ in the
NOUN

_____ section of (the) _____. Do you think you'll
ADJECTIVE   A PLACE

be able to support us by playing the _____? Do _____
NOUN   SAME NOUN

players make more than a thousand _____ a year?
PLURAL NOUN

Schroeder: When they have the musical talent of _____ or
CELEBRITY

_____, yes.
PERSON IN ROOM

Lucy: What are the odds that you and I will live happily ever after as

_____ and wife?
NOUN

Schroeder: Right up there with Beethoven giving me _____
ADJECTIVE

music lessons.

MAD LIBS® is fun to play with friends, but you can also play it by yourself! To begin with, DO NOT look at the story on the page below. Fill in the blanks on this page with the words called for. Then, using the words you have selected, fill in the blank spaces in the story.

Now you've created your own hilarious MAD LIBS® game!

UP ON THE ROOFTOP: DEEP DOG THOUGHTS

VERB ENDING IN "ING" _____

NOUN _____

NOUN _____

TYPE OF LIQUID _____

PART OF THE BODY _____

ADJECTIVE _____

NOUN _____

NOUN _____

PART OF THE BODY _____

ADJECTIVE _____

PART OF THE BODY _____

NOUN _____

CELEBRITY _____

NOUN _____

NOUN _____

VERB ENDING IN "ING" _____

When Snoopy's not busy being the World Famous _____
_____ VERB ENDING IN "ING"

_____, he can be found on top of his doghouse thinking
NOUN

deep random thoughts like this:

- Where is that round-headed _____ with my supper?
  NOUN

- I'd love a nice glass of _____ with my supper.
  TYPE OF LIQUID

- Why does Woodstock always fall asleep on my _____?
  PART OF THE BODY

- Should I hurl insults at that _____ cat next door or a cast-
  ADJECTIVE

  iron _____?
  NOUN

- If anyone asks me to chase a/an _____, I'll bite them.
  NOUN

- If I try to smooch that _____ lass Lucy on her _____,
  ADJECTIVE   PART OF THE BODY

  will she punch me right in the _____?
  NOUN

- I wonder if I should redecorate my doghouse in a/an _____
  CELEBRITY

  theme.

- If I could just publish one _____, I'd be the happiest
  NOUN

  _____ on Earth!
  NOUN

- Should I even get up today or just keep _____?
  VERB ENDING IN "ING"

Download Mad Libs today!

Join the millions of Mad Libs fans creating
wacky and wonderful stories on our apps!